W9-BIQ-908

03/2012

Animals in my Backyard

DEER

Jordan McGill

www.av2books.com

Go to **www.av2books.com**, and enter this book's unique code.

BOOK CODE

B 7 6 9 5 7 8

AV² by Weigl brings you media enhanced books that support active learning.

AV² provides enriched content that supplements and complements this book. Weigl's AV² books strive to create inspired learning and engage young minds in a total learning experience.

Your AV² Media Enhanced books come alive with...

Audio
Listen to sections of the book read aloud.

Video
Watch informative video clips.

Embedded Weblinks
Gain additional information for research.

Try This!
Complete activities and hands-on experiments.

Key Words
Study vocabulary, and complete a matching word activity.

Quizzes
Test your knowledge.

Slide Show
View images and captions, and prepare a presentation.

... and much, much more!

Published by AV² by Weigl.
350 5th Avenue, 59th Floor New York, NY 10118
Website: www.av2books.com www.weigl.com

Library of Congress Cataloging-in-Publication Data

McGill, Jordan.
 Deer / Jordan McGill.
   p. cm. -- (Animals in my backyard)
 ISBN 978-1-61690-936-9 (hardcover : alk. paper) -- ISBN 978-1-61690-582-8 (online)
 1. Deer--Juvenile literature. I. Title.
 QL737.U55M365 2012
 599.65--dc23
                         2011023412

Printed in the United States of America in North Mankato, Minnesota
1 2 3 4 5 6 7 8 9 0 15 14 13 12 11

062011
WEP030611

Project Coordinator: Jordan McGill Art Director: Terry Paulhus

Weigl acknowledges Getty Images as the primary image supplier for this title.

Animals in my Backyard
DEER

CONTENTS

Meet the deer.

He has large antlers.
He is called a buck.
Girl deer are called does.

He learns how to get away
from danger when he is young.

When he is young,
he lives with his family.

He grows new antlers each year.

Each year, his antlers grow bigger.

He eats plants with his tough teeth.

With his tough teeth,
he chews food quickly.

He smells with his nose.

With his nose, he knows
when danger is close.

He sees with large eyes.

With large eyes, he watches his front and back for danger.

He can run fast
with his strong legs.

With his strong legs,
he can jump and swim.

He lives in forests.

In forests, he can be safe.

20

If you meet the deer,
he may be afraid.
He could run at you.

If you meet the deer,
stay away.

DEER FACTS

This page provides more detail about the interesting facts found in the book. Simply look for the corresponding page number to match the fact.

Pages 4-5

Meet the deer.

He has large antlers. He is called a buck. Girl deer are called does.

Deer are mammals. Mammals are covered with fur or hair. A deer's fur is usually reddish-brown in summer. It is grayish in the winter. These colors let a deer easily blend into its surroundings. This helps the deer hide from predators.

Pages 6–7

He learns how to get away from danger when he is young.

When he is young, he lives with his family.

Baby deer are called fawns or calves. Shortly after birth, the doe quickly licks the fawn clean. This prevents predators from smelling the young. Males often leave their mother after one year. Females leave after two years. Before this, deer parents teach their young how to live on their own. They learn how to watch for and run from predators. When deer leave their parents, they are adults.

Pages 8–9

He grows new antlers each year.

Each year, his antlers grow bigger.

Deer are the only animals with antlers on their head. Often, only bucks grow antlers. Bucks shed their antlers each year. In the summer, they grow new antlers. If they eat plenty of healthy food, their antlers will grow bigger each year. A buck will crash his antlers against another buck's to fight for territory or a mate.

Pages 10–11

He eats plants with his tough teeth.

With his tough teeth, he chews food quickly.

Deer eat plants, such as herbs, leaves, and grass. A deer's stomach has four chambers to help digest this food more easily. In the first chamber, acids break down the tough plant fiber. Later, the deer will cough up the food, re-chew it, and then swallow it. The food then passes through the other three stomach chambers. Deer are fearful of predators. This causes them to eat their food quickly.

Pages 12–13

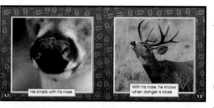

Deer have a strong sense of smell. They can smell predators from a long way away. They lick their nose to keep it wet. This improves their sense of smell. Their sense of smell helps them know if an area is safe. Deer also use their sense of smell to identify other deer. They can sense whether another deer is male or female and whether it is strong or weak.

Pages 14–15

Deer have large eyes on both sides of their head. This allows them to see in front and behind without moving their head. They watch for predators, such as wolves, mountain lions, and people.

Pages 16–17

A deer's body is adapted to offer protection from predators. Strong legs allow deer to leap 9-foot (2.7-meter) fences. They can swim 13 miles (21 kilometers) per hour. Deer can run more than 40 miles (64 km) per hour.

Pages 18–19

Most deer live in forests or near grassy meadows. Deer look for places that are surrounded by tall grasses, plants, trees, and shrubs. This protects them from harsh weather, such as rain or snow. It also hides them from predators. As people move into deer habitats, deer have difficulty surviving. People cut down the trees deer need to hide.

Pages 20–21

Deer are often found in parks and natural areas. Make loud noises to let deer know people are near. Deer should not be approached. People should not feed or touch deer. If a person encounters a deer in nature, he or she should back away calmly. Sudden movements can cause a deer to charge.

WORD LIST

Research has shown that as much as 65 percent of all written material published in English is made up of 300 words. These 300 words cannot be taught using pictures or learned by sounding them out. They must be recognized by sight. This book contains 47 common sight words to help young readers improve their reading fluency and comprehension. This book also teaches young readers several important content words. These words are paired with pictures to aid in learning and improve understanding.

Page	Sight Words First Appearance
4	the
5	a, are, called, girl, has, he, is, large
6	family, from, get, his, how, learns, lives, to, when, with, young
8	each, grows, year
9	bigger
10	eats, plants
11	food
13	close, knows
14	eyes, large, sees
15	and, back, for, watches
16	can, fast, run, strong
18	in
19	be
21	away, could, if, may, you

Page	Content Words First Appearance
4	deer
5	antlers, buck, doe
6	danger
10	teeth
12	nose
16	legs
18	forests